ON THE CAMPAIGN TRAIL

BIZARRE CAMPAIGNING

VIRGINIA LOH-HAGAN

 45TH PARALLEL PRESS

Published in the United States of America by Cherry Lake Publishing Group
Ann Arbor, Michigan
www.cherrylakepublishing.com

Reading Adviser: Beth Walker Gambro, MS, Ed., Reading Consultant, Yorkville, IL
Content Adviser: Mark Richards, Ph.D., Professor, Dept. of Political Science, Grand Valley State University, Allendale, MI
Book Designer: Frame25 Productions

Photo Credits: Prints and Photographs Division, Library of Congress, cover, title page; © Teresa Azevedo/Shutterstock, 5; © mpohodzhay/Shutterstock, 7; © vkilikov/Shutterstock, 9; Arnold Newman, Public domain, via Wikimedia Commons, 13; victorgrigas, CC BY-SA 3.0 via Wikimedia Commons, 17; George Rebh, CC BY 1.0 via Wikimedia Commons, 19; © rchat/Shutterstock, 21; © Andrew Cline/Shutterstock, 25; © Alexandru Nika/Shutterstock, 29; © SpeedKingz/Shutterstock, 31

Copyright © 2025 by Cherry Lake Publishing Group

All rights reserved. No part of this book may be reproduced or utilized in any form or by any means without written permission from the publisher.

45th Parallel Press is an imprint of Cherry Lake Publishing Group.

Library of Congress Cataloging-in-Publication Data has been filed and is available at catalog.loc.gov

Cherry Lake Publishing Group would like to acknowledge the work of the Partnership for 21st Century Learning, a Network of Battelle for Kids. Please visit Battelle for Kids online for more information.

Note from publisher: Websites change regularly, and their future contents are outside of our control. Supervise children when conducting any recommended online searches for extended learning opportunities.

Printed in the United States of America

ABOUT THE AUTHOR

Dr. Virginia Loh-Hagan is an author and educator. She is currently the Director of the Asian Pacific Islander Desi American (APIDA) Center at San Diego State University and the Co-Executive Director of The Asian American Education Project. She lives in San Diego with her very tall husband and very naughty dogs.

CONTENTS

Introduction 4

Chapter 1: **Kissing Babies (1833)** 8

Chapter 2: **Pig Joke (1896)** 10

Chapter 3: **Guts and Nuts (1964)** 12

Chapter 4: **Laugh Out Loud (1968)** 14

Chapter 5: **Nobody for President (1976)** 16

Chapter 6: **A Viral Look (2008)** 18

Chapter 7: **Vote Naked (2010)** 20

Chapter 8: **Witchy Candidate (2010)** 22

Chapter 9: **Demon Sheep Ad (2010)** 24

Chapter 10: **Rapping Grandma (2022)** 26

Do Your Part! 28

Glossary, Learn More, Index 32

INTRODUCTION

The United States is a top world power. It's not ruled by kings or queens. It's a **democracy**. A democracy is a system of government. It means "rule by the people." People **elect** their leaders. They choose leaders by voting.

Leaders **represent** the people who voted for them. They speak for them. They make decisions for them. That's why voting is so important. By voting, we choose our leaders.

Candidates run for **public office**. Public office is a government position. Candidates work hard to get votes. They run **campaigns**. They do this before an election. Campaigns are planned activities. Some campaigns are easy. Some are hard. And some are full of drama.

Campaign buttons are usually part of every campaign, even the most bizarre.

Candidates want votes. Candidates make posters. They send out ads. They give speeches. They talk to people. They shake hands. They meet voters. They share their ideas. They share their goals.

Some candidates will do anything to get votes. They lie. They steal. They cheat. They break laws.

Some candidates don't break laws. But they do **bizarre** things. Bizarre means strange. Some of these candidates won. Some lost. But we still remember their campaigns. U.S. history has many campaigns. This book features some of the fun ones!

Candidates must raise money. Campaigns are costly. Many voters donate money online to candidates.

CHAPTER ONE

KISSING BABIES
(1833)

Andrew Jackson (1767–1845) was the 7th U.S. president. He won the popular vote. The popular vote is the vote of the people. He spoke plainly. He didn't use fancy words. He met people. He was seen as the president for the "common man."

Presidential candidates are known for kissing babies. In 1833, Jackson went to New Jersey. He greeted a mother and her baby. The mother put her baby into Jackson's arms. Jackson said, "Ah! There is a fine **specimen** of American childhood." Specimen means example.

Jackson passed the baby to John Eaton (1790–1856). Eaton worked for Jackson. He kissed the baby. This started the tradition of kissing babies to get votes.

Andrew Jackson is on the $20 bill.

CHAPTER TWO
PIG JOKE
(1896)

William Jennings Bryan (1860–1925) was a lawyer. He was elected to Congress in 1891. In 1896, he ran for U.S. president. He was a great speaker. He used the new railroad system. He traveled by train. He visited many cities. Many people greeted him.

But not everyone liked him. Someone made a **stanhope** of him. Stanhopes are small objects. They have pictures inside. Bryan's stanhope was shaped like a pig. People looked through the pig's rear end. They'd see a picture of Bryan. "For President" is written on the picture. This poked fun at Bryan.

WORLD AFFAIRS

U.S. leaders must attend to world affairs. We're connected to what happens around the world. Other countries have political leaders. Deng Xiaoping (1904–1997) was the leader of China. He took over in 1978. China was a poor country. It was closed off from much of the world. Xiaoping made changes. He wanted to make China a world power. Today, China is wealthier. Many thank Xiaoping for this. He said "to get rich is glorious." This was shocking. Top Chinese leaders usually didn't promote wealth. But Xiaoping brought in a new China. People were inspired by his words. But there's no proof he actually said it. Some believe he didn't say it. But others do. A researcher said the slogan was only seen "in foreign reports." But it doesn't matter. Xiaoping is connected to the slogan. He did say, "To get rich is no sin." He did this on a TV show. There's proof of that!

CHAPTER THREE
GUTS AND NUTS
(1964)

Lyndon B. Johnson (1908–1973) was the 36th U.S. president. He was funny. He liked jokes. He liked telling stories. He had a big personality. In 1964, he ran for reelection. He ran against Barry Goldwater (1909–1998).

Slogans are catchy phrases. Goldwater's slogan was, "In Your Heart, You Know He's Right." Johnson's team thought that was silly. They came up with their own slogan. They said, "In Your Guts, You Know He's Nuts." They put Goldwater's face in the middle. They made pins. They made posters. They put out ads.

Johnson won by a **landslide**. This means he had most of the votes.

Lyndon B. Johnson was known as LBJ. He was a high school teacher.

CHAPTER FOUR
LAUGH OUT LOUD
(1968)

Hubert Humphrey (1911–1978) was a politician. He served as U.S. vice president. He also served in the U.S. Senate. In 1968, he ran for U.S. president. He ran against Richard Nixon (1913–1994). Nixon chose Spiro Agnew (1918–1996) as his **running mate**. Agnew would serve as vice president if Nixon was elected.

Agnew was unknown. Humphrey was more well-known. He made an ad. He targeted Agnew. Words appeared. They said, "Agnew for Vice President? This would be funny if it weren't so serious." A man was just laughing. That was the only sound. Voters liked the joke. But Humphrey didn't win.

THE IDEAL CANDIDATE

Ideal candidates are role models. Abraham Lincoln (1809–1865) was the 16th U.S. president. He's known as one of the best presidents. He was called "Honest Abe." He got this nickname when he worked as a store clerk. He gave people exact change. As a lawyer, he was known for being honest. In 1860, he ran for U.S. president. A journalist wrote a book about him. The book said Lincoln had studied Plutarch. Plutarch was an ancient Greek historian. Most students at that time read classic literature. Classic literature includes ancient Greek and Roman texts. The journalist assumed Lincoln was taught the classics. But Lincoln had never read Plutarch. He didn't want to mislead people. He wrote to the journalist. He said he wanted the book to be "faithful to the facts." He told the journalist he got Plutarch's books. He said he had now read Plutarch.

CHAPTER FIVE

NOBODY FOR PRESIDENT (1976)

The Youth International Party (YIP) was a **political party**. They were called Yippies. Political parties are groups. They organize campaigns. They help candidates win.

Yippies believed in free speech. They opposed government. They liked to perform. In 1976, they supported "Nobody" for president. They did this in 3 more elections.

They had many slogans. They said, "Vote for Nobody! Nobody keeps his campaign promises. Nobody deserves to live off your taxes. Nobody should run your business and your life. Nobody deserves your vote."

They made buttons. They wrote articles. They hosted a parade. Nobody was in a fancy car. Yippies were making a point. They thought nobody was voting. They wanted more people to vote.

Political parties have members. These members share the same beliefs. They share the same goals. The Yippies wanted people to get out and vote.

CHAPTER SIX
A VIRAL LOOK
(2008)

Mike Gravel (1930–2021) was a U.S. senator. He was from Alaska. He ran for U.S. president. He did this 2 times. The first time was in 2008.

In 2007, YouTube was still new. Gravel's team studied viral videos. Viral means shared widely. Gravel's team wanted to make a viral video. They had Gravel stare into the camera. Gravel did this for a while. Then he walked away. Next, he threw a rock into a small lake. He never said a word. Voters thought the video was weird. But they wanted to know more. However, Gravel was never elected president.

Gravel said, "Throwing a rock in the water was a **metaphor** for causing ripples and changes in society…" Metaphors are comparisons.

Mike Gravel never became president. But he did serve as both a senator and state representative of Alaska.

CHAPTER SEVEN

VOTE NAKED
(2010)

In 2010, Illinois wanted people to vote. The state changed its election law. It offered **absentee ballots**. Absentee ballots are mailed. They allow people to vote from home. People don't have to go to the **polls**. Polls are voting places.

Illinois voters have no excuses. They don't need to get dressed. They don't even have to leave the house. They don't need to wait in lines. An official said, "It is so easy to vote in the privacy of one's own home. One can even do it naked."

Some groups launched a campaign. It had a slogan. The slogan was, "Vote Naked Illinois!" They made funny videos. The videos showed naked voters. Objects covered voters' private parts.

Since the COVID-19 pandemic, more people vote absentee than they used to.

CHAPTER EIGHT
WITCHY CANDIDATE (2010)

Christine O'Donnell (born 1969) ran in several elections. She ran for U.S. Senate. In 2010, her campaign went viral.

In 1999, O'Donnell was on a talk show. She said, "I dabbled into witchcraft." She said she had a friend who was a witch. She said, "We went to a movie and then had a little midnight picnic on a satanic **altar**." Altars are sacred places for worship.

O'Donnell ran for office in 2010. This video was posted. People called her a witch.

O'Donnell then made a TV ad. She looked into the camera. She said, "I'm not a witch. I'm nothing you've heard. I'm you." This made things worse. People made fun of her even more.

HOT-BUTTON ISSUE

Hot-button issues refer to tough topics. People have strong emotions. They take sides. Candidates work hard for votes. Some will do shady things. Some might lie. They make promises. But they break their promises. Some even break laws. People want honest candidates. They check records. They do fact-checks. Some people think candidates should take lie detector tests. These tests show how people respond to questions. They check heart rates. They check blood pressure. They check breathing. They check sweating. But they're not always accurate. People taking the tests can get nervous. This may affect their results. Some people think lie detectors violate people's rights. People have the right to privacy. Many laws protect that right. In 2016, there was an online petition. Petitions are formal written requests. This petition demanded lie detector testing for U.S. presidential candidates. It had only 13 signatures.

CHAPTER NINE
DEMON SHEEP AD
(2010)

Carly Fiorina (born 1954) is a businesswoman. She ran for the U.S. Senate in 2010. She ran for U.S. president in 2016. She didn't win. But her campaign became famous.

In 2010, she made an ad. She targeted her opponent. The video was 3 minutes and 20 seconds long. It opens with sheep in a meadow. The sky gets dark. Lightning strikes. Scary music plays. A man appears. He's wearing a sheep costume. He has glowing red eyes. Fiorina said her opponent was a wolf in sheep's clothing. She called him a "demon sheep." The ad ends with, "Might there be a better choice?" The ad flashes to Fiorina.

The video was described as "bonkers." It was also called "one of the all-time great attack videos."

Carly Fiorina was in charge of Hewlett-Packard.
She was the first woman to do so.

CHAPTER TEN
RAPPING GRANDMA
(2022)

Linda Paulson (born 1942) is a mother. She has 5 girls. She has 4 boys. She has 35 grandchildren. She has 14 great-grandchildren.

In 2022, she ran for the Utah Senate. She did this at age 80. She made a video. She rapped. She did dance moves. Her daughter wrote the words. Her family recorded the video. They did it in Paulson's backyard. Paulson had a hard time staying on beat. But she had fun.

She lost. But her video was watched by millions. She made the news. She was talked about on talk shows.

FACT-CHECK

It's important to check facts. Facts must be correct. Here are some fun facts about strange campaigns:

- Voters compare candidates. They compare their ideas. They compare their work history. In 1884, Grover Cleveland (1837–1908) and James Blaine (1830–1893) both ran for U.S. president. People compared their head shapes. They compared their head sizes. Cleveland won.

- Mitt Romney (born 1947) had a dog. The dog's name was Seamus. In 1983, the Romney family went on a trip. Seamus was in a crate. Romney tied the crate to the car roof. He drove for 12 hours. The dog got sick. He pooped on the car. Romney ran for U.S. president twice. A group called Dogs Against Romney formed. They protested against him. Romney lost both times.

- Donald Trump (born 1946) became U.S. president in 2016. The total spending for the election that year was $14 billion. George Washington (1732–1799) was the first U.S. president. His campaign cost nothing. That was because he didn't do any campaigning.

DO YOUR PART!

U.S. citizens have 2 special rights. Only U.S. citizens can vote in federal elections. Only U.S. citizens can run for **federal office**. Federal office means a national office. It's different from state and local offices.

U.S. citizens have many other rights. But they also have duties. The most powerful is the duty to vote. Voting is how people choose leaders. It's how people make changes. It's how people promote their ideas. Those elected make the laws. They make policies. They make the rules. They work for voters.

U.S. citizens can vote at age 18. But people are never too young to get involved in democracy.

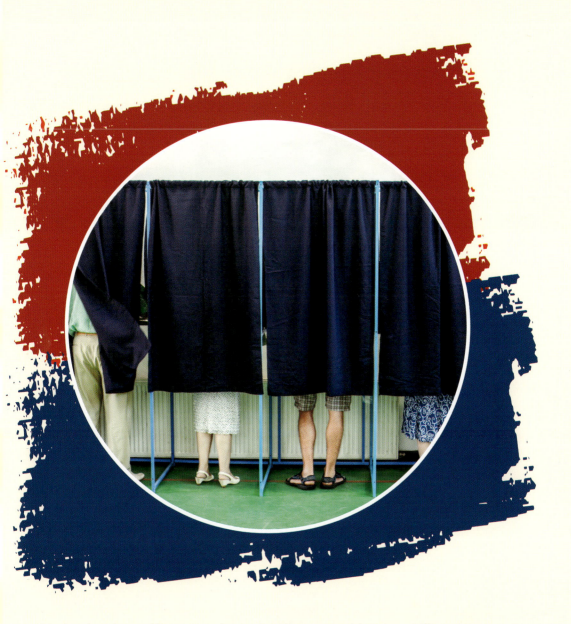

Voting is private. There are always booths or partitions at polling places.

Citizens must make good choices. They should vote for candidates who share their goals. They should look past the drama. They should find out what candidates stand for. Here are some ideas to learn more about candidates:

- ★ Think about the top issues you care about. An example is animal rights. Read about candidates. See if they feel the same way you do.

- ★ Attend candidates' events. Listen to their speeches. Write letters to them. Call them. Ask them questions. Get them to tell you what they think.

Everyone can do their part. Being a good citizen is hard work. But the work is worth it. Your vote is your voice.

Lots of information can be found online. Do a Google search.

GLOSSARY

absentee ballots (ab-suhn-TEE BA-luhtz) ballots completed and mailed in advance of an election by a voter who is unable to be present at the polls

altar (AWL-tuhr) a sacred place for worship

bizarre (buh-ZAR) odd or strange

campaigns (kam-PAYNZ) organized courses of action to achieve a goal such as winning an election

candidates (KAN-duh-dayts) people who want to be elected to certain positions

democracy (dih-MAH-kruh-see) a system of government led by voters, often through elected representatives

elect (ih-LEKT) to choose someone to hold public office by voting

federal office (FEH-druhl AW-fuhs) an elected position in the national government

landslide (LAND-slied) overwhelming majority of votes for one candidate

metaphor (MEH-tuh-for) a figure of speech that uses an implied comparison

political party (puh-LIH-tuh-kuhl PAR-tee) a group of people who have similar political ideas

polls (POHLZ) places where people go to vote

public office (PUH-blik AW-fuhs) government position established by law

represent (reh-prih-ZENT) to speak or act for another person or group

running mate (RUH-ning MAYT) a person campaigning with another person on a joint ticket during an election

slogan (SLOH-guhn) a short, memorable phrase used in advertising

specimen (SPEH-suh-muhn) an example

stanhope (STAH-nuhp) a trinket that contains tiny photographs and magnifying lenses

LEARN MORE

Books

Cunningham, Kevin. *How Political Campaigns and Elections Work.* Minneapolis: ABDO Publishing, 2015.

Goodman, Susan E. *See How They Run: Campaign Dreams, Election Schemes, and the Race to the White House.* New York: Bloomsbury, 2008.

Jenkins, Tommy. *Drawing the Vote: A Graphic Novel History for Future Voters.* New York: Harry N. Abrams, 2022.

INDEX

Agnew, Spiro, 14

Bryan, William Jennings, 10
buttons, 5, 17
campaign ads, 12, 14, 18, 22, 24
candidates
    campaign work, 4, 6, 8, 10, 12, 14, 18, 22, 24, 26, 30
    losing campaigns, 10, 12, 14, 18, 22, 24, 26, 27
    voter decisions, 4, 12, 14, 30–31
    winning campaigns, 8, 12, 27
China, 11
Cleveland, Grover, 27
costs of campaigning, 7, 27

Deng Xiaoping, 11

fact checking, 27, 30, 31
Fiorina, Carly, 24–25
Goldwater, Barry, 12

Gravel, Mike, 18–19
honesty, 15, 23
humor, 10, 12, 14, 20
Humphrey, Hubert, 14

Jackson, Andrew, 8–9
Johnson, Lyndon B., 12–13
jokes, 10, 12, 14, 20

kissing babies, 8

lie detectors, 23
Lincoln, Abraham, 15
naked voting, 20–21

Nixon, Richard, 14
"Nobody" for president, 16
O'Donnell, Christine, 22

Paulson, Linda, 26
presidential campaigns, 8, 10, 12, 14, 15, 24, 27
Presidents, U.S., 8–9, 12–13, 14, 15, 27
Romney, Mitt, 27

slogans, 11, 12, 16, 20

Trump, Donald, 27

viral videos, 18, 22, 26
voters
    campaigning to, 4, 6, 8, 10, 12, 18, 22, 23, 24, 26
    donations, 7
    voting, 4, 6, 16, 20–21, 27, 28–31
Washington, George, 27
witchcraft, 22

Yippies (Youth International Party), 16–17